NO MORE BANDAGES

"BECOMING WHOLE AGAIN"

LAKENDRA L. BODY

ACKNOWLEDGMENTS

GOD- I JUST WANT TO START OFF BY SAYING THANK YOU FOR LIFE. THANK YOU FOR HEALING ME, DELIVERING ME, AND ALLOWING ME TO BECOME WHOLE AGAIN. I WANT TO GO AHEAD AND THANK YOU IN ADVANCE FOR HEALING AND DELIVERING YOUNG WOMEN FROM HEARTACHES, HURT, ANGER, DEPRESSION, LONE-LINESS, MENTAL ILLNESS, AND PAIN. WITHOUT YOU I AM NOTHING, AND WITHOUT YOU I WOULD HAVE NEVER MADE IT THIS FAR. THANK YOU FOR GUIDING, PROTECTING, AND SAVING ME. I LOVE YOU AND I WILL ALWAYS PRAISE YOU FOR ALL YOU HAVE DONE FOR ME.

SHARON S. LEWIS- I want to start off by thanking GOD for such an amazing woman of GOD cousin, sister, and friend. Throughout a lot of my life experiences, you have been there encouraging, teaching, and instilling knowledge in me to become a woman of GOD just like you. The late-night calls, texts, and prayers have gotten me where I am today. Growing up from a little girl I had no idea you would be on the phone with me in my early adult years letting GOD use you to pray for me and my deliverance. BUT GOD! I just want to say THANK YOU! I love you and again I thank GOD for you.

TEMEKA JONES-DAVIS- Thank you for answering the phone when I needed a listening ear and thank you for not telling me what I wanted to hear. I am grateful to have a cousin like you that I can call anytime I need to vent or need encouragement. Most of all, I want to thank you for being there to motivate me through the tough times I had while trying to heal.

ERICA D. BOYD- Thank you for the motivational quotes and statuses you would post on Facebook about "WORTH" and everyday life things. It really helped on my worst days. Thank you for encouraging me to publish this book even in the times that I wanted to give up. Lastly, thank you for being an amazing teacher, and role model for young women. The status you would often post about letting it hurt to let GOD heal you. I just want to say that I have done just that.

MOM- I just wanted to say, "Thank you for being an amazing mom." Thank you for raising me, teaching me, nurturing me, and being hard on me. Back then I could not understand why you were strict and didn't want me to attend certain events or hang around certain people. NOW, I fully understand. You did an amazing job raising me but it was up to me to continue what you taught. Despite me slipping, I just want to say I love you and I apologize for not taking a lot of your advice but being an adult in the real world has taught me a lot. I know the things in this book will be heartbreaking or new to you, but I have to be obedient as GOD has delivered me and instructed me to do so.

DAD- Despite our rocky relationship in my teen years, I thank GOD for growth and understanding for the both of us. I thank you for being extra hard on me. I needed all of that and more. As kids we fail to understand the tough love and the strictness, but as adults we realize that it was only because you wanted the best for us. Thank you, Dad, for your tough love.

GRANDMA VICKEY-Thank you so much for encouraging me and praying for me each and every day. I know for sure you will read my story because you love to read, but I just want to say I'm sorry for not opening my mouth while going through everything alone. I did not have the gut to even discuss how bad loneliness had taken a toll on me to the point where I was doing things that I did not realize I was doing. BUT GOD! Is a good GOD and he delivers us to a point where we can share anything, we endured that he had to deliver us from.

MAINMAN-Things have been so rocky without you, but thank you for instilling GOD in me and the qualities of life. Most of all thank you for the great wisdom you left me with. Thank you for staying the course and encouraging me to FIGHT, PRAY, AND PRESS my way through every circumstance or obstacle I may face. Lastly, thank you for getting on your knees in front of all of us. Proverbs 22:6 Train up a child in the way he should go: and when he is old, he will not depart from it is now in full effect.

GLADYS LEWIS- The first night I met you at work and you told us how many jobs you had to make ends meet, I knew then we would click. Thank you for never sugar coating anything to me. Thank you for being straight up with me, and teaching me how to stand my ground to say NO when I kept trying to see the good in others. You always told me that I needed to take time out for LAKENDRA and that you sure was right.

LAST BUT NOT LEAST MRS. SHARON DIANE TATE-JONES- I have no idea why GOD led me to you for advice that day but I'm glad he did. Thank you for taking out the time to let GOD use you to Pray, encourage, and prophesied to me. Despite of me slipping up and getting disturb GOD still made a way and allowed me to understand today. Everything you told me has been adding up and giving confirmation to me. Continue letting GOD use you. A true beautiful woman of GOD.

I dedicate this book to all of the young and old females who have settled for less than they deserved. I want to encourage you to stop filling the void after every relationship and heartbreak. Give yourself time to heal. Start with your own happiness, seek GOD to become whole again. Ask him to heal your broken heart, and most of all speak that you will be renewed and restored back to where he need you to be. YOU ARE ENOUGH! YOU ARE A QUEEN! DO NOT LET NO MAN TREAT YOU LESS THAN YOU DESERVE. Lastly, do not continue to cover your heart with bandages, they are only temporary for open wounds.

This is based on a true story, names in this book have been changed due to the respect of others.

On January 17, 1998 a beautiful 7pound 8ounce beautiful baby girl was born. Her aunt helped her mom name her LAKENDRA LAVONSHAE BODY. That little girl was me. I was raised in a family home by the same hard-working man who helped raised my mom which was her grandfather and my great-grandfather. It was love at first sight when he held me for the first time, and from that moment on, I never let him go. He raised me from a little girl to a grown woman off of nothing but love. Branching off into the real world I mistaken lust for love, allowing every guy to gain my trust. When I finally began to realize my worth, my heart felt as if it would burst. GOD took me through these situations to encourage women, young and old, to not cover heart breaks with bandages. He put it on my heart to tell you to allow yourself to heal before jumping right into another relationship. Let him heal you and make you whole again. Do not be so quick to find a replacement. Seek GOD, find time for yourself, love yourself, do what's best for you, and it will work in your favor and for your good. Do not get caught up in temptations trying to fill voids by allowing other men to come in your life, when you are not healed from the last man. I am a witness. All of that will only make things worse. No matter what I did, who I slept with, who I dated, or how they treated me, I still could not enjoy the moment and live my best life because I still had a broken heart. It took me eight years to realize my worth. Seven years to love myself. Six years to realize I needed to be healed. Five years to realize that you cannot trust everyone with your heart. Four years to realize that no matter how much you love someone, they can and will turn their back on you, and there's absolutely nothing you can do but suck it up and keep moving forward. I had to learn that everything happens for a reason, and that reasons cause change. Sometimes it hurts, Sometimes it's difficult, but in the end it's all for the best. Never stop trusting and believing in GOD and the plans He has for you.

YOUNG AND VULNERABLE

*I*t all started on a hot, sunny, summer day in May. School had just been released for the summer, and I was passing to the 6th grade. I was so proud of myself. Growing up my parents were strict, so I had to have someone with me wherever I wanted to go. This particular day I asked could I walk to the park. The answer was yes, but I had to take my little brother along with me.

He was just a toddler at the time. I strolled up town holding his hand just as happy as I could be. Even though he was with me, I felt free. Approaching the laundromat en route to the park, I noticed two guys parked at the car wash staring at me. I continued walking by holding my brother's hand as if I didn't see either of them.

Before I could pass by the vehicle they were sitting in, the guy on the passenger side begged for me. I hesitated of course, but then he said, "I'm not going to bite you". Because I knew him from around town, I trusted just what he said. I went up to the truck, still holding my brother's hand and asked, "What do you want?" He then asked me for my phone number.

I was skeptical about giving it to him, but anxious to see what he wanted, so I gave it to him anyway. I proceeded to walk to the park. When I arrived there, I let my brother play around, and I went over to sit on the bench. Sitting there I realized what I had just done- I had given a GROWN MAN my number. Before I could think it all the way through, I was getting a restricted call.

It was him. I answered and his first question was, "How old are you?" I said "Thirteen." He told me not to tell anyone that we had talked. Being naïve, I said "okay." He made me promise not to tell anyone. Not thinking much of it, I said, "I promise." He then goes on to telling me how beautiful I was to him and how he wanted to make me his little baby. He ended the conversation by telling me to remember his number instead of saving it as a contact in my phone and he will talk to me a little later. When I hung up from him, I had butterflies and I was scared at the same time. I knew I was too young and he was too old for me.

Being young and vulnerable, I tried it out just to see how it would be. Talking to him turned into months and then became years. He had a girlfriend, they lived together, and he was a father figure to her kids. GOD forbid, what would happen if anyone found out about us. The phone conversations we had were amazing. I could not believe a GROWN MAN was so into me, because in school none of the boys liked me. All they did was bully me and call me names. The girls practically did the same by making fun of me because I didn't have a big butt like theirs or a little boyfriend like them.

The first couple of weeks of conversation I fell in love with him. I loved everything about him, from his half talking to his missing tooth. I would sit on the porch daily just to see that white Navigator pass by. Just seeing that it would put me in a good mood. He would catch wheels and spin tires just to show off in front of me, no matter where he saw me at or no matter who I was with. He was in a relationship but dared me to talk to anybody else, not even the little boys in the same grade as me. I was so young and dumb that I did just as he told me. I can remember going on a Student Council trip in school and he told me to get a shirt spray painted that said "DA BOSS LADY." He wanted me to wear it to the Catfish festival that was coming up in a month.

I got the shirt spray painted and I wore it proudly that day. The shirt was red with black writing, and I wore black tights with red Converse to match. When he saw me that day, he was smiling ear to ear because he couldn't believe that I had done just as he asked me to do.

MISTAKING LUST FOR LOVE

Three years had passed, we had not touched or seen one another physically. Basically, we fell in love over the phone over the few years. The phone conversations were all we had and he had me wrapped around his fingers. Year three came and we still were conversating without anyone knowing but him and I. This was the year I built up the nerves to tell one person. My late cousin, Kathy Grace Smith.

My secrets were always safe with her. The both of us would walk uptown just so I could see him pass by me. At this point our parents had gained a little more trust for us and we would go walking every day. One day I built the nerves up to ask him for money. His only response was, "How are you going to get it?" We all planned to go into the store where he dropped the money on the floor, and I walked behind him to pick it up as if I had found it. The moment he did that, my mind was falsely mistaking that he loved me. Fast forwarding to the end of that year, I got comfortable enough to kiss him. For some reason my cousin and I were out walking at night. When he saw me, he called me and before I could say anything, he was carrying on about how good I looked.

He then asked for a kiss. I was nervous but I said yes. We ended up kissing on a corner down from where he and his girlfriend lived, without no one seeing us but my cousin because she was with me. As his lips approached mine, he was handing me money at the same time. I knew in my heart, what I was doing was wrong.

In my mind, I had it going on and he was all mines, but in reality, I was being his side piece the entire time. I didn't know if he was a man or a woman, but he was on to something. By this time, I had turned sixteen. I was so into him, that you still couldn't pay me to talk to another male. Time passed and I started to get up on game and knowledge. I felt like a fool being loyal to him and he lived with another woman. I begin to ask myself, *who do he play me for?* Or *Who do he think I am?* From thirteen to sixteen I matured and most of all, I learned a lot about life. One thing I learned was not to be nobody's fool. I finally started to talk to other guys but I made sure that he did not find out. I continued to play along like he was my only one, because I was scared of the way he may act if I told him that I didn't want to continue anymore after three years. During our time of talking, I did not act any different around my parents nor did I let it affect my education. I no longer cared about what the boys or girls in my class said about me anymore. I knew at that moment, I was good enough to have anyone I wanted, after being attractive to a grown man. Each day I went to school I was so happy, nothing and no one could take that away from me. I began to glow and step my game up, and the same boys who called me names wanted to be my boyfriend and the same girls who bullied me, wanted to be my friend.

HUMILIATED

The next year approached, we were still going strong, with no one knowing but my late cousin and us. All of a sudden, he wanted to introduce me to his long-lost friend. I told him that we did not need anyone in our business, but he told me that it was okay to tell him and he would not say anything. I trusted just that. He wanted me to meet him in person, but I told him that he could introduce us over the phone.

Days after we discussed that, they pulled up on my cousin and me walking uptown by the carwash. There were only a couple of people at the carwash, but as cars started passing by, I told him it would be best to call me on the phone. It wasn't two minutes before they pulled off and he called me. He told me that his friend wanted to speak to me. I told him that it was okay.

A deep voice on the other end of the phone said, "Hello, my name is Daniel, but they call me Candy Licker." I didn't know anything about a candy licker but the song that was out by Marvin Cease. I told him OKAY, and that my name was Lakendra, but he could call me Kendra. He then went on to ask me had I ever sat on a nail before? I told him no. He asked if I would like to sit on one? I told him, "No." He laughed and then said that it was nice to meet me.

I said nice to meet you, too. He had taken my brain for the loop the rest of that day. All I could think about was why would he ask me a dumb question about sitting on a nail. The next day he called me saying that his friend wanted to be hooked up with my cousin. I asked my cousin if she was interested, but she told me that Daniel was not her type of guy because he had piercings in his eyebrow, lip, tongue, and at the top of his ears.

Days had passed but I didn't hear from him, so I called his phone and learned that it was disconnected. Before nightfall, a number showed up on my phone that I had never seen before. I answered and it was him. He called me from Daniel's phone to inform me that he was having problems with his girl, and she had cut his phone off. He would be using Daniel's phone until he was able to get his back on.

He and Daniel started to hang together more to the

point where, he called me every single day three weeks straight. After those three weeks, it went back to me not hearing from him at all. I built the nerves up to call Daniel's phone just to see had he heard from him but he said he hadn't seen him in a while or heard from him. Instead of Daniel hanging the phone up, he began to go into conversation with me. While conversing with him, he told me that I didn't need no one like his friend, who takes his relationship problems out on me.

Daniel told me that I needed someone who loved me. He told me that I needed to be with him because he could love me better than his friend ever has. I hung up at that moment because I knew that was not the right thing to do at all. I had no way of telling him that Daniel was no friend to him. He only wanted what he had. Day after day Daniel blew my phone up begging and pleading for me to talk to him.

After not hearing from his friend in months, I was heartbroken. I lowered my standards and gave Daniel a chance. He knew just how to comfort me in my time of need. I fell for it because I was lonely and didn't have anyone else. Daniel introduced me to phone sex and sending nudes to him. I knew it was wrong, but I continue to do it for the pleasure and enjoyment. There's a saying that says: *If you do wrong, wrong will follow you.* That is a very true saying.

Daniel and I would have phone sex almost every morning, and he would want me to send him a picture of every part of my body. We went strong for a month or two until he got intoxicated, and left his phone unlocked. Unfortunately, his girlfriend went through it. She found all the nudes that I had sent him. Instead of her mentioning it right then she waited good until she and him got into an argument to mention anything about it. One day she saw my mom at the store getting food and she told her about the nudes she had found on his phone. When my mom arrived back home from the store, she rushed in the house and asked to see my phone. She went into the bathroom with it, and she began talking to someone.

I had no idea what was going on until she asked me had I ever sent nudes to Daniel. At first, I lied, and then I thought of the saying, *"The truth will set you free".* I went on and told the truth. Everything that was done in the dark, had come to the light and I needed GOD more than I ever had before. My mom was beyond upset. I could see the anger brewing in her eyes. She left me standing there and she went to Daniel's house. She asked him personally what was going on, and he blamed everything on his friend. He told my mom that his friend was using his phone to communicate with me and the nudes I sent were for him. I hadn't had any contact with the friend in nearly 6 months and I could not believe Daniel had put the blame on him.

Next, my mom pulled up on his friend, but he had no idea what was going on. Which he didn't because he thought things between us had been over. Things started to get real, and I told the GOD'S honest truth about everything, from the beginning to the end. Now the both of them were in it together, one could not blame the other. My mom called my dad to notify him of what was going on, and he told her to take me to the police station. When we got there, my mom told the officers what was going on. They then asked me to write a statement.

They told my mom there was nothing they could do because I had not had any sexual contact with either of them. When we left the police station, she took me home and there was my dad waiting for us. We all went into the house. He gave me a lecture and he whooped me for the very first time. The next day I woke up humiliated.

I felt so ashamed. At that moment I just wanted my life to end. I had disappointed my Mom, Dad, and most of all, I let my Grandmother down. My mom took my phone away for an entire year. The rest of that year I lived in hurt, humiliation, and shame. Around that time, I went through life avoiding anyone who I assumed knew anything about it. I would avoid going places, because I thought everyone knew what had gone on. My dad took my sisters and I on a trip to Geyser Falls, but I was so uncomfortable. I walked around unhappy with my head down thinking the people there knew exactly what I had done.

As time passed, I sent messages by people to apologize to Daniel's friend because he had nothing to do with what me and Daniel had going on at that moment. I deeply felt that Daniel was no type of friend to him because friends don't snitch on friends. True friends automatically take the blame. A year after all this was over, I saw the both of them riding together like nothing had ever happened. The crazy part about it is that he still looked at Daniel as his friend.

EXPECTING ME FROM SOMEONE ELSE

*Y*ears passed and before I knew it, I was graduating from high school. I had blossomed into a beautiful, smart and such an intelligent young lady. My maturity was at its best and I had learned a lot from my past. Around this time, my love life was everything. I was dating this guy by the name of Don. Don was quiet, shy, respectful, sneaky but most of all handsome.

He graduated two years prior to me, and he was older than me but none of that matters because I liked them a little older than me. Don and I fell deep in love the first few days after meeting one another for the first time. Around that time, he asked me to be his girlfriend. I said yes and gave it a try. He was the best thing that had ever happened to me in the year of 2015. He started college at Mississippi Valley State University and decided it was not for him.

Later I encouraged him to get a job so that he could make some money. He did applications everywhere, but the fish house was the only one who called him to work. I was so excited the day he told me he had gotten the job. His work journey began, and I felt like I had finally found someone I could spend the rest of my life with until I learned that he smoke marijuana. My heart was crushed, because he had hidden it from me, but I continued to love him the same. Arguments started to occur between us because I started to feel unappreciated.

We ignored the red flags and solved all those arguments with sex. We went 4 years strong until one Valentine's Day he showered me with gifts, but wanted to spend time with his homeboy instead of spending quality time with me. I begged him the entire day to spend quality time with me, but he refused to. I had given him a card with $20 in it and I wanted it back after being upset about him refusing to spend time with me. He had his homeboy bring him to my grandfather's house where I was. He came into the house and threw the card at me.

I was pissed because my grandfather had just fallen sick. Despite him being asleep when all of that took place, I still felt like Don disrespected his house. Of course, we made up , but that only made things worse. All of a sudden, he quit his job because he had gotten into an argument with one of his co-workers. That was a major turn off for me because I could not believe he was letting someone run him off of his job.

I had begun to believe that he just did not want to work at all. Eventually, we started to grow apart when he told me he was moving away from Belzoni and relocating to the Gulf Coast. Around that time my grandfather's sickness had gotten worse, so I knew moving three hours away wouldn't be good for me being that I was his caregiver. Don and I tried a long-distance relationship, but it didn't last a month. We decided that it was best that we go our separate ways. At first, I was devastated and heartbroken until I got an inbox from Mike. Mike and I had been chatting on and off since I was 8th grade. He never made a major move because he knew I was so much younger than him.

We always talked about getting together when I got older. The moment he messaged me, I thought that moment was our chance. He had waited that long for me; I just knew he had to be the one. Mike was handsome, independent, high in confidence, and hardworking. I knew he had a history of females, but I trusted that he had changed. One day he invited me to his house and when I got there, I was so nervous, but tried to act as if I was not. He showed me around, then and later we sat down on the sofa. I was uncomfortable at first because he had a pet cat, but after he locked the cat up in a room, I felt comfortable.

We couldn't have a decent conversation without him starting to come on to me. Before I knew it, we started to make out and ended up in his bedroom with my clothes off. It was a shame how he did me, I could not explain. He made me feel as if it was my first time. What Mike had given me was something I had never had before. He gave it his all while I stared at the picture of his son and baby mama hanging on the bedroom wall.

When we were done making out, I could not keep myself together at all. My body felt like I was high off of a drug. I was so knocked off of my feet, I texted him that entire night complimenting him on doing such a great job. We made out three more times after that until he realized I had caught deep feelings for him. He started to ignore me, and I had no idea what I had done wrong. I wanted to be in a relationship and spend the rest of my life with Mike but Mike didn't want the same thing from me.

I wanted to spend time, build, bond, and most of all have a family, but Mike only wanted one thing. After not hearing from him in weeks, he finally reached out to me and told me that he only wanted sex from me. He made it clear that he didn't want no strings attached. I was vulnerable and, in such denial, I still gave it to him knowing that was not good for me at all. I had caught feelings for him that he had never had for me.

I agreed to give it up to him with no strings attached like a fool. He paid attention to the things I would ask him for after sex for example: to hold me, cuddle with me, and kiss me. He began to pull away from me again. I was trying to love a man that only wanted what was between my legs. He got to the point where he would fool with me when he got ready, and I settled for that not knowing my worth. At times I felt used so I told him that he would have to start paying for me to come over to his house.

We continued for a while until he asked me to do a porn video with him. I instantly lost all my cool for him because he had gone way too far. That was our last time being acquainted, of course things went left. He would send me harsh messages talking about how my body was made wrong and how he just wanted sex from me because I was never his type of woman. That put a big hole in my heart. I would have evil thoughts about harming him and destroying things that belong to him, but I stayed humbled. I did not seek revenge because I knew eventually, he would reap what he sowed. My mind was puzzled at the way he talked about me after making love to me.

Mike had talked about me to the point where my self-esteem had become completely low. In my mind, I thought I was not good enough for any guy around. As days passed, I asked GOD to bind every feeling I had for him out of me. I asked him to bind the soul-tide that Mike had left upon me. I ask GOD to deliver me from all the insecurities I had about my body that he had instilled in my head. Last but not least, I asked GOD to help me forgive Mike for everything he had done to hurt me. The saying *"life goes on"*, was better said than done back then but I had to do just that if I didn't want to get hurt again. There were times when temptations came in, I would get lonely and end up texting him just to find out he was the same Mike that he was back then.

I gave myself a month to heal then I was ready to try again with another guy, but this time I made the move instead. I was desperate for anyone that I could find. I met John through Facebook messenger. At the time I felt like he was heaven sent. We conversed for a week, and he invited me over to his house. I thought he had cooked dinner and wanted to surprise me with an in-home date, but instead I was his dinner.

I left his house clueless and feeling like a new woman. He treated me like a queen and spoiled me with everything I possibly wanted. He had gone out of his way to prove his love for me, and I had to repay him. After our first time being together, I could feel a change in him days after. I did not expect that out of him at all, but he showed me who he really was. I started to hear things around town about him. I questioned him about it, and he lied each time. There were times when I thought he was innocent every time. As things started to unfold and come to the light, I knew then none of it was a lie. He meant so much to me. Despite what I had heard about him, I decided to accept his flaws and believed he would change. Three years later, I was at my breaking point with him.

I had had enough of him making love to me and ignoring me days after. That had begun to be a trend for him, but I was too blind to see it. It took him making a baby with my friend's mother for me to halfway wake up and smell the coffee. I was broken because he lied about it when I asked him. He told me he hadn't had contact with her in a year, but I knew that was a lie.

We continued to, but I was not feeling him anymore. We made an agreement that if the baby came out to be his, we would go our separate ways, but if not, we would start new. The baby came out to be his, and guess what? I accepted all four of his kids and continue to love him for who he was. CRAZY RIGHT? It was not love; it was lust. Not to mention the soul-ties he had upon me that made me go back each time, when I knew he was not good for me mentally.

Later, we got into a disagreement, and he decided

that we should be friends instead of having relations. I could not take the fact of him reminding me of us being just friends, so I gave up on him again. I moved on with my life but every time something didn't go right in my love life, I went running right back to him. The last chance I gave him, he ruined it. I noticed that he didn't care for me, like I cared for him; he did not treat me the same as I treated him.

It had gotten to the point where I had to beg him to do things that he knew he was supposed to do. The way I felt about him was unexplainable. He could hurt me so bad, and the same night he could make love to me and change my mind just like that. He could do some major tricks with his mouth that made me feel like I was in a different world. Every week on my two days off and even nights after working an 8-hour shift, we would make out.

He had gotten so comfortable to the point where he trusted me to shave his head. He even told me his overall body count. He then begins to share with me how he had stripped for some ladies in my hometown. I could not believe what I was hearing, but that still didn't change the feelings I had for him. John was originally from Gary, Indiana, but he lived in Little Rock, Arkansas before he decided to take on a job as a Deputy Sheriff in Humphreys County. I came to realize that I was in love with a man that had too much pride to admit that he loved me just as much as I loved him. At times I could tell when he was fighting his feelings for me.

We went strong until he took a trip to Little Rock, Arkansas to visit his family. He came back brand new; he had completely lost his mind. I heard from him that Sunday when he arrived back in town, but after that there was no sign of him. His phone went to voicemail the rest of that week. There I was again back in the same boat. Heartbroken! I was so hurt. I revealed one of his darkest secrets. I did not care or think about the outcome or circumstances. I had let him know that I was not to be played with. When I finally got a hold of him, he explained that he was dealing with his emotions and needed time to think to himself. I always told him he could never hide anything from me, because eventually I would find out. It wasn't two days later that I found out he had his second baby mama pregnant again.

He was waiting for his 5th child to arrive, and lord knew it was time for me to leave. I came all the way to my senses then. I learned my lesson the hard way. Ignoring the red flags had FINALLY come to an end. I was giving my all to a man who wanted his cake and wanted to eat it too.

He was not my man, and he never had a desire to grow old with me. The only time he spent with me was inside the bedroom, and some nights in the meeting room, when he was on duty. It's crazy how I was blind to so much of his mess. He never loved me, he just loved what I could do for him. After being hurt so many times by John I was completely fed up, but most of all I was in a dark moment of my life. One day I can remember going over his house to chill and things got real. I don't know how we ended up on the subject of the Bible, but that's where we were at that moment. We went back and forth about Christmas and holidays being in the Bible, and that's the moment I found out he was a Jehovah witness. Not judging based on his religion but that just shows you that I had been obsessed with a man for over four years and I had no idea of his religion. That disagreement led to a heated moment, and I left his house but what he said stuck with me for the rest of the day. I just could not believe what had came out of his mouth. Nevertheless, that still didn't change the way I felt about him. I kept going back every time.

The soul-ties he left on me had me feening for him like a drug. It was so bad to the point where I had to get it prayed off of me. We were still talking on and off after that, but we were not sleeping around. One day he told me he was getting married and he asked me what I thought of the person he was getting married to. I could not believe he was getting married to her. I knew her so well and I also taught her kids in daycare. The only thing that made me accept the fact that they would match because of the same religion. We slept together twice in December and by May, he was at the altar saying I do. Today I thank GOD for delivering me from such a mess I had gotten myself into, after I ignored every sign he had given me to leave it all alone.

TRUSTING THE WRONG PEOPLE WITH MY HEART

Being off and on with John, I always kept a friend on the side. There was this one that I never really took seriously. His name was Marvin, but everyone called him "Duck". I had known him for quite a while. He liked me, and I liked him, but we never got serious. His skin tone was high yellow, he had pretty brown eyes, and he was on the heavy side. His size did not bother me at all because his face appearance made up for all of that. We met one night at the Mexican restaurant. Before then I knew he had his eyes on me, but I just wanted to wait until the right time to acknowledge it.

I looked at him as a friend, but he would contact me as if we were more than friends. He would send me a message every morning pouring his heart out to me.

One day the pattern of the messages began to stand out to me. I started to think about how serious he was, but I still could not get John out of my system. I was still battling with the soul-tide he had left on me. Dealing with a situation like that, you had to be strong enough to break an unhealthy soul tie.

I was weak as I could be. I always let my body make the decision for me instead of my mind. No matter what I did, I could not get over John. There were times I thought about the way Marvin was pouring his heart out every day begging to be with me. I told myself, "*You got someone right in front of you, trying to love you.*" Then I would ask myself, "*Why are you settling for less?*" I made a decision to cut John off and I started to get acquainted with Marvin, the one who had love, time, patience, and attention for me.

Marvin lived in Isola, Ms., but we would meet at his Dad's house a couple of streets from my Grandfather's house. We never chilled inside of the house because we wanted to respect his elderly Grandmother. His Dad owned a mobile home that sat right in front of the house. That was our chill spot. On weekends Marvin would invite me over, we would cuddle, watch tv, and have the best talks ever.

We both would vent about past hurts and cheer one another up. The mobile home had everything in it that

we possibly could need: beds, a Tv, bathroom, air condi-
tioner, heater, refrigerator and more. My trust issues
were all over the place around this time, but I built up a
little trust just for him. Our relationship was going so
good until a game was played on Facebook on his brother's page. The game was fun and simple, all you had to
do was send a picture of your crush to his inbox and he
would post it on his Facebook page. I sent a picture of
Marvin as my crush. His ex-girlfriend sent a picture of
him too. She was the same ex he always vented to me
about how wrong she had done him. Minutes later, she
inboxed me, questioning me about a man that was not
hers. I immediately called him and told him about it but
he told me to look over her, and not to let her come
between us. That didn't sit well with me. I was always
taught that if a woman approaches you about a man,
that man still has something in common or something
going on with that woman. Instead of going back and
forward with her, I decided to send her all of the screen-
shots of him pouring his heart out to me. She could not
stand that at all. Instead of us continuing to argue about
him, she talked about me instead. I was at a stopping
point until she said I wiped old people's butt for a living
and she heard I was living off of my Grandfather's insur-
ance check. I read her all of her rights because my
career and my Grandfather didn't have anything to do

with what we had going on. I think I offended her calling her everything but a child of God, so I guess she called him crying to him about it. He called me going all off about what I had said to her. He had lost his ever-lasting mind. He was taking up for her like she wasn't the one in the wrong. I hung up on him because I could not believe him. Minutes later, I received a text from him being called a messy wh***. I was hurt because I had never gotten a reaction like that from him before and I was pissed because she was the one in the wrong but he was blaming everything on me. I accepted the fact that it had happened, and I blocked both of them then continued on with my life.

Months later, I was strolling Facebook and found out she was pregnant, that was the moment that everything had added up. When he found out she was pregnant he had to figure out the fastest way to get rid of me before getting caught up. That game with his brother hit the nail on the head. From that moment on, I never spoke to him again. That heart break led me right back to John. Being that John had so much going on and did not have time to comfort me, I went searching through my inbox for guys that I always ignored. There I found Reginald. He was basically a sugar daddy who had been hitting me up for years, but I never paid him any attention because that was not who I wanted. When things got tough and I got lonely, I decided to try him out. Reginald was tall, handsome, muscular, and he drove a yellow Camaro. He had been married before, but at this time he and his wife had separated. Reginald was a wealthy truck driver and he was popular too. We started talking as friends because I didn't accept the fact that he was still married. I told him he had to get a divorce in order for us to be in a relationship. We started to spend quality time together, but I was not pleased with it because it was always inside of his 18-wheeler at night. I began to question him about his feelings for me and the only thing he kept bringing up was the way his ex-wife had treated him. Oftentimes I had to remind him that I was not his ex-wife, but I had to suffer from the treatment she had given him. I tolerated it until I was fed up and I realized that was not what I wanted at all, especially after he had begun to be a bitter old man and his spirit did not set right with me. At that moment I decided to be alone to let myself heal from all of my past hurt. I did not talk to anyone. I started to be focused on school more and most of all my Grandfather's health. During 2017, I had actually gotten used to being alone and not talking to anyone. I was at ease with my past hurt, and I refused to let anyone steal my joy. October 28, 2017, my grandfather took a turn for the worst, and he passed away from congestive heart failure. Anybody that knew me, knew also how much my Grandfather meant to me. He was my everything. After taking a major loss I drifted off into a dark, lonely place in my life. I wanted to give up on life again, but little did I know it was my Grandfather's time up on earth and not mine. GOD still had a purpose for me and that's why I'm still here today sharing my story with you.

BELOW MY WORTH

*S*ix months later, I received an inbox being asked to go on a date with a guy that I had no idea had intentions of dating me. His name was Joshua. Joshua was handsome, anointed, smart, and most of all, he was a gentleman. Joshua lived alone in the white folk's part of town in Belzoni. After something came up and we weren't able to go on the date, he cooked dinner and invited me to his house instead. He had everything laid out followed by a surprise massage.

He had candles, towels, oil, and rubbing alcohol. He had really out done himself with this date. I had never had a man massage me before. Of course, I was instantly hooked. He took his time and massaged every inch of my body. There was no better feeling. I had never felt that good before in my life. The massages and dinner continued once a week for three months and after that we fell deep in love. After falling in love, he began to act like he was scared of commitment. He ignored my calls and left me wondering, *"Where did I go wrong?"* Times after that he would invite me over but stand me up as soon as I pulled up to his house. Standing me up had begun to be a trend for him. After he had done it so many times, I became fed up with it all. He had turned me into a devil because I felt as if he was standing me up and leading me on for the fun of it. I have never been the type to hurt anyone or even had the gut to, but one night he had pushed me to the limit. That was a night we were supposed to meet, and I caught him buying marijuana from a marijuana man. I knew I had to be seeing the wrong thing. The Joshua I know, church going Joshua, anointed Joshua, true colors had finally come to the light. Who was I to judge? I was so surprised at what I saw. We went back and forth for four years, breaking up and making up. During those four years I found out his deepest flaws, he smoked cigarettes, marijuana, and drunk liquor every day. He was a totally different person at home than he was at work and at church.

.   .   .

I was totally fed up with the person he was pretending to be, so I moved on with my life after being led on and lied to plenty of times. I decided to take a major break from relationships again. Six months later I got an inbox on Facebook from an old high school friend asking to take me out on a date. Being that it had been so long since I dated someone, I decided to give it a try. NOTICE! I never gave myself a complete year to heal, I just moved right on to the next one. This person had been right in my face for years, but I never gave him the time of the day. His name was Billy; everyone called him white but in reality, he was mixed. His Dad was black and mom was white. Their family was known to be wealthy because his Dad owned a farm that was passed down to him at an early age. Word around was everybody he had been with in the past only used him for his money. I was not that type at all. I work hard eight hours a day and earn my own money. At this point, I just wanted something real. I wanted to settle down, be free from hurt, and have my own man. Billy took me out on a date and after that, things got a bit more serious. I thought he just wanted to be friends like we were before until he asked me to be his girlfriend. I was totally shocked, but that's the moment I knew it was time that I cut Joshua and everyone else off who was constantly playing games in and out of my life. I asked Billy to give me time to clean things up and I would let him know when I was fully ready to be his woman. It did not take me long at all, because I did not want Billy to slip away from me. The new year was approaching, and I did not want to carry that baggage with me into another year. I had seen on Facebook where people plan to write down everything and everybody they did not want to take into the new year on a piece of paper and burn it. I decided I would do the same thing. When it was time to write down my people and things, John's name was the first name on the list on my people section. I had gone back to him time after time year after year and it was still the same exact thing. After burning him off things took off with Billy and myself. We started to spend more time together and do new things. Every other weekend we were in a nice hotel in Jackson, Ms. living our best lives. I just knew I had found my true love. We were so in love. He even proposed to me on my birthday. I was finally happy and getting ready to marry the man of my dreams. It was so unbelievable to me. He was all I had ever dreamed of in a man until we spent this one weekend in Jackson, and he took sick on me. I had never drove in Jackson, Ms., but at this point I had to face my fears and get him to the nearest clinic or hospital because he was running a fever and didn't look good at all. When we arrived at the clinic, he gave me his phone to contact his mom to tell her what was going on. While I was doing that, he was getting checked in. After hanging up from his mom, a message thread popped up on his phone as if he was recently on it. The messages I read nearly gave me a heart attack. I viewed the profile of the person he was chatting with, and I could have turned that place upside down. At that moment every feeling I had for him left and I wanted to kill him in that clinic, but I stayed humbled because he was not worth my freedom. I waited good until he got well, and I threw it to him. He constantly tried to explain but that was not good enough for me at all. He had plenty of sad excuses, but none of them worked being that he was chatting with someone with the same sex as him. He told me that they had been talking way before we started dating and he ended up talking to this guy because he was lonely. He came clean with me discussing every detail, but I told him I preferred him to be talking to a woman when he got lonely instead of a MAN. This was a different type of hurt and humiliation for me. I shared the situation with his mom before sharing it with anyone else because I knew how much faith she had in us. After telling her, she was so deep in denial that she cursed me out and blocked me on Facebook. She also told me, *"You are supposed to love a person, regardless of what they have done"*. I don't know what world she had been living in, but I refused to walk down the aisle before GOD and marry a man that I knew was involved with someone as the same sex as him. To be sure I was not breaking things off too soon, I contacted the guy through messenger to be sure of what was going on. The guy gave me more than enough information to RUN AND NEVER LOOK BACK. Yes, I was hurt, broken, busted, and discussed but GOD had my back the entire time and I truly thank him for that. It took a lot for me to get over the situation, because I never thought in a million years that something like that would happen to me. Literally, I drifted off into a slight depression mode, but with my faith in GOD I got through it. Everybody was on the outside looking in, trying to figure out what was going on but eventually it came out. There I was lonely, miserable, depressed, and last but not least, I had become vulnerable once again. I knew Joshua had gotten news about what had happened with Billy and myself after reading a long message he had sent me about becoming a better man for me.

EMPTY AND LONLEY

I gave in to Joshua's apologies and a year later, we got our own place together. Getting my own place was something I had been wanting to do for a while. The first couple of months of us living together was amazing. He treated me like a queen. He cooked for me, ran my bath water, did the laundry, paid the bills, cleaned the house, and got me everything I wanted. All of a sudden, the pandemic came about, and things went downhill. He started back drinking and smoking heavily. Being that I worked in a healthcare facility, he didn't want to kiss, touch, or hug me. It had gotten to the point where I had to beg him to sleep with me. I worked the evening shift and he worked the morning shift so every night I came home to him sitting on the porch smoking, drinking and treating me like a roommate. This one particular night, I had gotten completely fed up with it. The next day when I went to work, all the things crossed my mind about what we were going through. I decided to text him and I told him if things didn't get any better than I was going to move on with my life. When I got home that night, he was packing up, so I decided to help him since he was leaving a lot of things behind. While packing his dishes in the box, he goes to the living room and destroys everything on the wall. When he finished destroying everything, he got on the phone, called my mom and told her to come over to get me like I had done something to him. When my mom walked in the door, she cursed and asked what was going on. When I told her what was going on she called the police. The police arrived about fifteen minutes later, but his sister was there with a stick in less than two minutes. I had so much anger in me that I could have fought both of them and been ready for whomever else. The police told us that we had to make a decision who would stay at the house that night. Joshua said he wasn't leaving, and I also said the same thing. We went back and forth for ten minutes until my dad arrived and persuaded me to stay overnight at my mom's house that night until things cooled down. The plan was for Joshua to be out of the house by morning so I could come back home. The stay at my mom's house that night was a nightmare. I was so upset I could not sleep at all. I was in a hurry to get back to my own house. The next morning came and it was time for me to go back home. When my mom and I arrived, Joshua was still there sitting in the dining room with his feet up smoking a cigarette. That really made me hot because he was supposed to be gone when I arrived the next morning. At that point, I didn't know what to do. My mom suggested that the best thing to do was go to the landlord. The landlord said he had never experienced such before with a tenant, so he turned everything over to his daughter and she gave us the option to get it together or get out. Being that this was my first time being out on my own, I did not want to be embarrassed about getting evicted out of a house I put so much into. She gave us until 2:00pm that day to make a decision. I asked Joshua if we could work it out, but at that moment all he thought about was keeping the house for himself. What we had didn't matter to him at all anymore. After going back and forth about who would keep the house, he finally gave in and told the landlord's daughter to give him a week to be out. During that week, we slept in separate rooms for seven days. We did not speak at all. We communicated through texts messages. During that week I received a gift in the mail from him each day. In my mind it was him making up to me and I thought he would stay but later he sent me a message saying he bought me all those things to start a talent with, so I can make more money to front the bills because he knew I wouldn't be able to do it on my own. The seven days were up, and he moved out a day before it was time to pay the rent. He thought he was hurting me, but in reality, he was helping me. The day he decided to move all of his stuff out and leave, I was at work. I didn't know he was actually going to leave. It was around 4:30pm, I started to feel sick at work. I went to the bathroom and before I could sit down on the toilet, a big hunk of blood fell out of me. I immediately called my supervisor and told her what happened. She told me to go get myself checked out. I went to the hospital, and they could not find anything wrong. When I left there, I headed home with such a heavy heart. When I arrived home, he was sitting at the table calling around trying to find someone with a truck. When he finally found someone, I begged him not to leave and he was still packing while laughing at me cry and beg. Harsh, right? When two guys arrived to move his furniture, I got in the bed and covered my head. Meanwhile, he unplugged the tv, took the fire stick, and told me I could have the broke down bedside table. At that moment, I just knew that I would have to have some type of help or counseling. The pandemic stopped all of that and the only person who could counsel me at that moment was GOD. I was so broken, I thought I would never come out.

TRYING NOT TO FILL THE VOID

Months later, I felt at ease. I was at peace with living alone and I slept well every night until I started to give myself to people who I didn't know. GOD was healing me, but the devil came in and made the process feel long and hard. I started to fill the void and that was the last thing I wanted to do, but thanks to loneliness and temptations I did it anyway. Every three weeks I was with a different guy who I thought could take the pain away, little did I know, they were taking my faith, my worth, and my soul away. At that moment I realized I had a mental illness and a split personality. KEN B was telling me to have a pity party every time, but LAKENDRA LAVONSHE BODY was telling me not to put myself in those same positions that GOD was trying to heal me from. After having sex, touching, kissing, and cuddling. (Fornicating) With that person I still felt the same, but I didn't notice the pattern until the hurt and soul ties started to build up. All of it caused depression and hurt. A place I never wanted to be buried in anymore. There were many nights that I thought I would lose my mind suffering from depression and loneliness. I wanted to be whole again, but there was Satan in my mind telling me my heart was not strong enough for the healing process.

REALIZING MY WORTH

Five months later, I decided to cut everyone off I had dealings with to completely heal. When I did that, I instantly became lonely again. I suffered from loneliness on a daily basis. Loneliness had led me into thinking Facebook messenger was a dating site. I would sit up and scroll through the people I may know looking for the guy who could be that special one. I would sit up and inbox guy after guy thinking I would find my happily ever after. I never had any luck, unless I was down to give it up. All of them would say "I'm chilling" or "I'm not ready to be in a relationship" and there was lonely me settling for whatever they could give me. Suddenly, all of it began to drain my energy to the point where I asked GOD to help me realize my worth. I asked him to take away loneliness and help me to become whole again in every prayer I prayed. There were times where I felt like he was not answering my prayers, but the problem was I was not putting in the work and allowing him to come in to heal me all the way. Every time I got on track, the devil would send something or someone to throw me off. Suddenly, I became unavailable to text messages and calls from people who expected me to settle below my worth. I had my guard all the way up and my heart covered until one day an old friend decided to come back into my life. Demond the one I had puppy love with in the 5th grade. There I was again being distracted. We hadn't talked in years being that he had resided in Houston, Texas after high school. When we started back talking, I could feel the same feelings I had for him before. Although he stayed in Texas, he always came to Belzoni to visit his family on certain occasions.

He had lost a loved one in his family around this time, so he made it his business to come by and see me. I invited him over and as we sat on the couch and talked, I shared with him about the bad break up I had with Joshua. He then asked me if there were any bills at my house that needed to be paid. I told him I needed him to pay my light bill for me. He asked for my cash app and he sent me the money for that bill. At that moment, I logged into the website to pay my bill right in front of him. I didn't want him to think I was lying or using him. I was smiling from ear to ear because I had never had anyone to just come out and do such for me before. I was the one used to doing all of the giving. We talked a couple of more minutes and then lust and temptations came. We started making love on the sofa and ended up in my bedroom. The same feelings I had for him back then were the same feelings I had right then. As soon as we finished, he was in a hurry to go. There I was back at square one lonely and heavy hearted. (NOTE: THE VOIDS ARE ALWAYS TEMPORARY) He told me he would come back the next day before he leaves and check on me but there was no sign of him at all. He waited until he got back to Texas to call me. Days passed before I came to my senses and realized it was just for the moment. I decided again that I would be single and just wait on GOD. I always heard my aunt say, "*FAITH WITHOUT WORK IS DEAD*" and that is a true saying. See, I had the faith to become whole again, but I was not praying and opening up to GOD like I should have been. Every time I got on a journey praying to GOD, something would come to distract me. It would be an old ex, temptations, lust, the devil,or mental illness. I would let any little thing bother me and disturb my peace.

LONELINESS

Staying by myself got tougher every day. It got to the point where I just felt like I had to have someone. At times it made me feel as if I was losing my mind. I then started to use Adult toys to fill the void and cover the wounds. When one didn't work how I wanted it to work, I would purchase another one. When that got old the devil had my mind just where he wanted it to be. He put in my mind that I just had to have someone laying next to me at night. There I was again searching for anybody that I could think of to be that special one for me. I was thirsty! I was desperate! I was making myself look like a fool instead of letting GOD heal me completely to be ready for the man of GOD that waits for me.

. . .

I searched and I searched! I ended up with men all the way from Jackson, Ms. letting them in my house, letting them sleep in my bed, use my tub, and my bathroom. How crazy could I be with the crime rate so high in Jackson, and I didn't know a thing about either of them. (GOD, THANK YOU FOR PROTECTING ME.) I am not ashamed to tell any of it because that is not what GOD wanted for me, that's what the devil wanted. He wanted me to continue to be hurt, he wanted me full of soul ties, he wanted me bound, depressed, and desperate. He wanted me to fight those demons that were not mine. To make a long story short, I was so focused on finding the right one that I barely gave GOD any of my time. As I just typed that I cannot believe it at all. (GOD FORGIVE ME ONCE AGAIN.) See the devil had me thinking that was all I needed: A MAN! Someone to have sex with. Someone to hold me at night. Someone I could show off on Facebook to get likes, loves, and comments. (TO BE HONEST, MY TEENAGE YEARS WOULD HAVE BEEN SO MUCH BETTER WITHOUT FACEBOOK). None of it worked out for me because most of them were not of GOD. Not to judge anyone, but it was the truth. Upon meeting guys on social media, I didn't do a background or a religious check. I just gave them my number, asked for their name, conversed for a couple of days and there I was with them in my bed. I didn't take time out to get to know either of them for who they really were and had no idea what was to come ahead of me from them.

BATTLE BETWEEN GOD AND THE DEVIL

One day while still going through this, I felt really hungry and I decided to fix myself some home-made burgers. While fixing the burgers, I was listening to a lady pray on Facebook. She prays every Wednesday morning. I would always catch the rebroadcast. When the burgers were done, I went to my room and sat in my recliner chair. I started to eat my burgers while still listening to her pray. Before I could finish my burgers, the Holy Spirit hit me and tears began to flow down my face. I began to think about the way I had been feeling. The loneliness, slight depression, disappointment, and rejection. Then I began to think about how loneliness and hurt had made me so bitter. To me, I was such a nice and caring person. To the guys who used me, rejected me, or hurt me, I was the devil to them. See I was praying to GOD for blessings with the same mouth I was tearing them down with, and that was not good at all. I decided to try one last time by inboxing this guy and it worked. He was old enough to be my granddaddy, but he assured me he would be good to me and he didn't even know me. His name was Earl. We exchanged numbers and we began talking from there. He said he knew some of my people and he worked with a few of them. Every night he would come and see me at the nursing home where I worked and he would call me on every break he had at work. He was the sweetest thing I had ever met. He told me how he had been hurt in the past by a young girl he had been dealing with for years who only used him. I knew exactly where he was coming from because I had been used numerous times before already. We went strong for a month. I hid him because I didn't want anyone to know our business. This one particular day he came to my house and when he was leaving out of the back door, he noticed my prayer wall. He started looking around and I began to tell him all I had been through and the purpose of me writing my first book. He looked kind of shameful, but kissed me goodbye and went on out the door. Later I tried calling him to see if he made it home but he did not answer. He did call me back and he explained to me that he didn't want to do the relationship thing anymore. He told me that he was a registered sex offender and I was a good woman. He felt that he didn't deserve me because he was still stuck on the female that hurt him in the past. There I was hurt and broken again, I could not believe what I was hearing. I could not believe he had just given up on us that quick. I mean we had just started to work on something together. I was back in the same boat again. As I stated above, I know things would have been so much better now if I had not involved myself with social media at a very young age, but everything happens for a reason.

I would seek revenge when I was hurt by a guy by tearing them down, but GOD was the only revenge I needed. I was hurting and ruining those guys deeply with my harish words and I didn't realize it. I was misused, and hurt so much that I thought it was okay to do it to others, because I wanted them to feel the same pain I felt. Each time I was hurt I really never allowed GOD to heal me. I was on to the next every time, filling the void and covering past hurts. There were times where I said Enough Is Enough! And I still went back to doing the same thing adding more hurt and allowing more soul ties to come upon me. There was this one night I prayed and cried out to the Lord. I was so broken! I said, "Lord, no other man will get in this bed until I am married." See the devil knew what I had told GOD and he knew if I stuck with GOD completely that he would not win and he wouldn't have any more parts in my life. Sadly, two weeks later someone else was in my bed, that was not my husband. I had told myself that I would not have any dealing with this person anymore. Nevertheless, I decided to give him a second chance. He explained to me that his Dad had fired him from his job, he didn't have a vehicle, nor any income coming in. He said he wanted to get himself together to come be as one with me. I had never been the type of woman to let a guy ride in my car or stay with me for free, so I told him he had to work on that part before we made any other move. We began conversing and I started to let him come to my house to see me. The first time was great. But the second time he showed up intoxicated, with a strong smell of liquor on him and a really hot temperature. He came in all hostile, pants sagging and before I knew it, he had his hands around my neck. I was so scared because I had never experienced anything like that before. I just knew that he would abuse me at any minute. BUT GOD was with me and I am so grateful for that. I pushed him about three or four times until he realized how serious I was, that's when he stopped and said he was just playing. I demanded for him to get out of my house. He attempted to leave, but came right back begging me to have sex with him. Being that was all I was used to, I let him get on top of me anyway. The feelings were not there at all. To be honest, I was praying to GOD that he got off of me. While laying there, I could feel GOD working on me and on the other hand he was wondering why I just laid there. Of course, it was a turn off to him and finally he got up to leave. I was so happy. I told myself that I would never put myself back in positions where GOD delivered me from and that's what I meant. Loneliness and mental illness will ruin your life. I am a true testimony. These things will make you think you're losing your mind. All alone I was suffering from it, but had no idea what was going on. I was walking around like I had it all together, but I was losing it. I would pray and do good one week, but the next week I was distracted by something, somebody, or pleasure. Pleasure was a way for me to fill the void as well but after pleasuring myself, the pain would still be there, the hurt was still there, and I needed to be healed. I didn't know my worth. I needed guidance. I needed a piece of mind, but I never allowed myself to be filled or equipped with any of it. Every time I drifted back off searching for someone instead of waiting on GOD to send me the one, he made just for me. I didn't have any patience at all and the devil had taken every piece of faith I had. I got to the point where I would go a few days without praying or giving GOD my time. I would work, cook at my dad's club, and go home. Mostly every day I was miserable. I was tired of being rejected and unwanted. Satan had me just where he wanted me at until one day GOD woke me up to equip me how to fight the devil with a whole armor of him.

hile home alone, a traumatic event happened to me that changed my life forever. See, when GOD wants to heal you, he knows just how to stop you in your tracks. Despite that situation coming from the devil to steal, kill, and destroy I had to be reminded who my GOD was. I had to be revived, renewed, and filled with the holy spirit. It was time that I had to repent and rededicate my life to Christ. I had to be who GOD called me to be instead of who Satan wanted me to be. In other words, I had to stop running from my calling, my anointing, and my gifts. I had to learn to keep a whole armor of GOD over me at all times, so I could be able to handle and fight every demonic spirit or obstacle that may come my way.

I had to get in my word, I had to believe it and most of all I had to stand on it.

In conclusion, I just want to THANK GOD again for protecting me during those times and guiding me as I was going below my worth. I was letting Satan get a hold of me being with

several guys and going through things I had no business going through. I know for sure I will touch someone, speak to someone, save someone, and most of all minister to someone through this book. It's okay to mess up. No one is perfect, but be sure not to repeat the same mistakes over and over again. Get a closer relationship with GOD. Lastly, repent! It is never too late to ask GOD to forgive you for your sins. He will wipe all of them away and give you a fresh start. For example, being whole again. It does not matter if you have had sex before marriage. If you want GOD to send you a husband. Repent! Remain celibate. Ask him for forgiveness. He will take it all away, and give you what your heart desires. It starts with you staying focused, not getting distracted, staying faithful to GOD, and doing the right things. While doing that GOD will fulfill every promise, destiny, goals, purposes, and dreams he has for you.

TAKE THE BANDAGES OFF AND HEAL!!

Made in the USA
Columbia, SC
12 February 2024